How to live for "nearly" free
How to survive when you've hit rock bottom

Not a Dime

.

Table of contents

    Housing
    Food
    Clothes
    Transportation / Car Care
    Child Care/ Pregnancy
    Utilities
    Healthcare
    Education
    Entertainment
    Income/ Banking/ Credit
    Christmas/ Thanksgiving
    Miscellaneous : food items for non-food uses
    Miscellaneous

    This Christ centered resource manual is a must have for nonprofit agencies, churches, single parents on a budget, and for those who simply want to learn how to stretch their dollars.

Housing

I was about 9 years old, my family was evicted. I remember sitting out in the street in a chair in the freezing cold that night. I remember the thin blue blanket over my head, covering my body as I sat in the metal fold out chair. My feet was numb as I saw all our furniture, bags, food & boxes scattered out in the yard. I didn't understand what was going to happen or why it happened but the memory is forever etched into my mind.

Proverbs 24:3

"Through wisdom is an house built; and by understanding it is established".

- Stay out of low income areas! The wait lists are longer, the quality of whatever is available is lower and the section 8 wait lists are probably closed. INSTEAD research and find the highest tax bracket city, suburb, and town next to the area you wish to live & seek out resources there. Areas with more money generally have more resources to offer those in need. Locate the helping agencies in these areas. The food pantries, the local DSS office, and ask for a list of local family shelters.
- Call the local elementary school, ask for the guidance counselor or school social worker and ask for a warm referral to any income based apartments or family shelters I the area. Get the name of the person to ask for. Call more than one school. Explain that you are "displaced". Shelters often require multiple calls per day. Ask for an appointment to be considered for a room.

- USDA Rural Housing- income based housing in rural areas. Google USDA rural housing apartments. Get the name of the complex, google search for the direct number and property manager name. Explain that you are displaced (with kids if you have them) and have whatever extenuating circumstance. Ask what you would need to provide with your application to obtain an apartment as soon as one is available?

- For the Habitat for Humanity program applicants must have good credit, must live in the area for 1 year, and call in advance for all the guidelines. Fix your credit and income prior to applying. They check all 3 bureaus.

- Www.craigslist.com search " room rentals" in the city you wish to go

- www.socialserve.com search by rent amount, income, zip,

- Section 8 low income housing voucher www.affordablehousingonline.com/open-section-8-waiting-lists

- Create a calendar for when to apply for the specific Section 8 programs
- Typically rental agencies that rent to section 8 voucher holders offer lower rental cost units to those who are cash paying. For example you may find a 4 bedroom cheaper with one of these companies than with a realtor that does not rent to voucher holders.

- Get on wait lists early, if you know you plan to move get on wait lists 2-5 years in advance!

- Buy a family sized tent and set it up on a friend or relatives land. (Can't have kids) Find heating & cooling sources.

- Get a FREE house
1. Check with your local city Real Estate Division, Master in Equity Sales
   Homes are taken by the city for unpaid taxes. Homeowners abandon them and they end up at
   auction. If no one bids on them at the auction then they will

go to the real estate division. If they sit unsold long enough the city will sometimes give them away. If you find one of these properties run a title exam for liens and be prepared to make significant repairs.

2. Find a REO realtor, Real Estate Owned or bank foreclosed property. After a property has sat unsold for a long time and had many price reductions the lending institutions will want to cut its losses and just give the property away free. You may still have to pay property taxes but the house will come without liens. Sometimes an owner after learning their house has little to no value and actually cost them money to unload because of commissions and fees a good REO agent will offer to find them a buyer free of charge that will take the property, costing the owner nothing. These properties will probably have tax and or water liens.

Food

I must have been around 13 or 14, when I learned what starvation felt like. It was around the end of the month when the food stamps had run out and there was no income until the 1st. We had no food. I remember being so hungry at night before bedtime that I went to the fridge and ate a bowl of ice. I sat and looked out the window at the street light and I crunched on that little brown bowl of ice. I'll never forget that.

1 Timothy 4:4-5 For every creature of God is good, and nothing to be refused, if it be received with thanksgiving: For it is sanctified by the word of God and prayer.

- Save fast food receipts for free food survey rewards
- Google kids eat free in your area
- Call united way and Salvation Army for a local list of food pantries
- Call these pantries to inquire what documentation is needed to obtain food
- Make a food pantry calendar
- Call local large churches and ask if they are having any community events like movie nights that will provide food, make a calendar
- Check the newspaper for non- profit events that include "free food" key words
- Call local radio stations for a list of upcoming promo events that will offer free food
- Free snacks? Take apartment tours for cookies, popcorn and soda
- Call local food co-ops and ask to be on their donation list for unclaimed orders
- Summer government school meal programs
- Free snacks? Go to Publix
- Several restaurants offer free meals on your birthday (Denny's, Captain D's, Hooters, I hop, Ruby Tuesday, Steak N Shake, Texas Road house, Zaxby's) Call for details and

participation
- Chic-fil-a cow day, Krispy Crème free doughnut day, and more
- Grand openings of new restaurants in the area, pizza and burger places are the best
- Bookit program.com- free pizza for students
- Oneharvest.com
- If you have AAA use this discount for food such as with Papa John's 25% off 25AAA online only

Clothes

When I was about 11-12 yrs. old we lived in a blue house on a hill, we were poor. I didn't have a closet or a dresser. I remember having a large black trash bag with clothes in it. Smelly, ill-fitting used clothes was what was in the bag. I vividly remember a pair of off white corduroy pants that I would wear for 2-3 days in a row. I wore them because they fit. I remember being teased, made fun of, and called stinky and ostracized by my classmates. It hurt. The kids did not understand and as a child I could not control the situation.

Nehemiah 9:21 Yea, forty years didst thou sustain them in the wilderness, so that they lacked nothing; their clothes waxed not old, and their feet swelled not.

- Local clothes closets, arrive an hour early
- Shop at thrift stores in higher tax bracket zip codes, the clothing quality is often better
- Ask thrift stores if they use vouchers and if so what organizations issue them?
- Some local shelters or domestic violence shelters may have clothes closets, call and ask if they are open to the public
- Always shop off season, and save it back. Do this especially if you have children.
- Print store coupons and sales paper coupons before going
- Ask friends and neighbors for clothing referrals from kids with similar sizes
- Shop on ebay
- Go to yard sales in higher tax bracket zip codes
- Look for quality, and materials that will last long

Utilities

Oh the joy when you discover your utility deposit has been credited to your current bill.

Exodus 9:29
And Moses said unto him, As soon as I am gone out of the city, I will spread abroad my hands unto the LORD; and the thunder shall cease, neither shall there be any more hail; that thou mayest know how that the earth is the LORD's.

- Most Electric companies offer free or discount energy saver light bulbs
- Life line link up free government cell phone service
- Call your electric company and ask the customer service rep which local charities they see providing electric bill credits
- LIHEAP Energy assistance program
- Time Warner Cable ask for the ELP internet option for $14.99,
- Once you have internet get a Skype number for home phone service or a google voice number for a local alternate number
- Buy your modem at Wal-Mart or Amazon to avoid the modem rental fee
- Use 4 wic candles with a mirror behind it for extra free light
- Use a small toaster oven, and crock pot instead of your regular oven and stove top for most meal preparation, this will save on your bill
- Use a grill, cook outdoors electricity free
- Unplug everything at night or when you are away
- Get a phone book and call local churches and ask for the requirements for their benevolent fund utility assistance
- Get a local helping agency list from food banks, or DSS, or Salvation Army this will list who provides utility assistance
- Use fans instead of the AC or use Fans during the day and the AC at night
- Wash clothes on cold
- Insulate all your windows and doors

- Turn down the heat and invest in electric blankets

Healthcare

I realized one of my worst fears as a single parent when I became too sick to care for my 3 kids and there was no one to care for me. God, cartoons, and good neighbors like Ms., Lori, Ms. Tiffany, Ms. Yvette, Mr. Lynn, Ms. Dianne, and Ms. Barbara got me through that time in my life. Without having to ask, food and medicine was dropped off at my door.

Jeremiah 33:6 Behold, I will bring it health and cure, and I will cure them, and I will reveal unto them the abundance of peace and truth.

- Create your own medicine/ health care bag
- In this bag or box you may want to include bandages, burn kit, finger splint, Neosporin, Tylenol, aloe vera, anti-diarrhea medicine, toothache supplies, tweezers, gauze, heat pack, ice back, blood pressure checker, blood glucose checker, tourniquet, eye drops, matches, cough medicine, thera flu, vix, a thermometer and anything else you may need.
- Google free health clinics in your city
- Go to the ER if you must but do not give your SSN, these charges will be placed on your credit report if you cannot pay
- If you do provide your SSN then immediately ask for the hospital charity forms
- Free birth control from the health dept.
- Check out herbal remedy books from the library or research online
- Black seed oil, and coconut oil are staples for many remedies
- Print pharmacy coupons prior to buying things at Pharmacies
- Google pharmacy discount cards and sign up for them!
- Google free adult or child dental clinics in your area, call the local health dept. or other dentists and ask if they know of any
- When calling health clinics ask if they offer a " sliding fee"

scale
- Google " New Eyes for the Needy" and " Lions Clubs" in your area
- Even if you cannot pay always have some cash for the minimum required co-pay at some facilities

Child Care/ Pregnancy/ Kids

Dedicated to Mt Horeb UMC Mothers Morning Out program. Jennifer & the staff was my saving grace during my time of life's reorganization. They afforded me the time I needed to get my family on the right path as well as forged a lifelong impact on my 2 youngest children at no cost. I could not have gotten this far without your support.

Psalm 127:3-5

Lo, children are an heritage of the LORD: and the fruit of the womb is his reward.

- Call local pregnancy centers for diapers and supplies at least 3 months into your pregnancy. In some cases there may be prerequisites to obtaining the donations. You may have to watch videos or read books to "earn" items.
- Yard sales in high end zip codes that list " baby items" for sale
- Call thrift stores and ask what days will they have their half off sales, buy baby items then.
- Aldi and Dollar General are two of the lowest cost places for diapers & wipes
- WIC offers FREE breast pumps just ask
- Call area hospitals for car seat programs. Start early at least by 3rd month of pregnancy there may be a waiting list
- Search for " sliding scale" day care centers
- Get on your states child care voucher wait list as soon as you are able to apply after birthing your child. The wait list can be 2 plus years long!
- Call and ask which of your states Medicaid programs offer circumcision
- Call your local Catholic church and ask for the catholic charity in your area devoted specifically for women & kids

- Apply for mothers morning out & parents morning out programs, ask for scholarships
- AWANA offers scholarships
- Scholarships for local children's theaters and museums call and inquire
- Girl Scouts & Boy Scouts offer scholarships
- Get 2 free toys per month at the Home Depot and Lowes. They offer Saturday craft days for kids, call for the dates
- Christmas program angel tree sign ups start in SEPTEMBER! Call to get on wait lists then!
- Call food pantries and ask for baby diapers and wipes. They often have these items and no one asks for them.
- Sign up for your states TANF program, they may pay for child care while you job search and after you find work if you qualify

Transportation/ Car Care

I remember shortly after being homeless and moving into our new apartment the engine in my Ford Explorer blew up. So in the dead of winter we walked. Me, my 1 year old in her stroller and my 6 year old. It was humbling, we bundled up and walked in the freezing rain at times to get our groceries and home supplies. For 3 months we walked and rode in the local taxi. A few times we were given rides. I remind my children of this experience, to always be grateful and appreciate the fact we are blessed to be riding, and safe, and warm.

Proverbs 16:9

A man's heart deviseth his way: but the LORD directeth his steps.

- If it is in your budget and your credit is acceptable apply for an auto care/ gas credit card for gas and car repair emergencies.
- Call local helping agencies for gas, and bus voucher qualifications
- Craigslist carpool ads
- Before getting any car maintenance or repair go to the company website and PRINT their coupons!
- Use grocery points for gas discounts
- Go to a manual car wash or fund raising car washes
- Invest in a small VAC and water hose and bucket and never go to the car wash again! DIY at home
- Use the cheap gas locator app
- Murphy oil may still offer 3 cents off per gallon when paying with a Wal-Mart gift card
- Invest in car repair how to DIY books from e-bay or free at the local library
- Keep an emergency car kit in your trunk, flares, orange triangle, tire pressure indicator, flash light, fix a flat etc....
- Invest in an AAA membership for towing discounts, lock outs and more
- Call local helping agencies for "free car" programs – usually prequalification's may include being employed for a certain period of time, a minimal deposit, references
- Amtrak $5 Summer travel deals in state for kids

Education

In October 2007 my first child was due and it was also my last semester of Graduate school. I took my laptop with me to the hospital and got to work! Since I'd heard labor induction would take several hours I literally finished everything up just before the real pain began. I know that the 8 years I spent in study was not in vain, there was a reason for all things.

Proverbs 18:15 The heart of the prudent getteth knowledge; and the ear of the wise seeketh knowledge.

- Free online classes
- Free classes offered at the library, and local community colleges
- Free classes at local Adult Education facilities
- Certification programs for under $200 at local community colleges: Notary public, Life/ Health Insurance and many more.
- Free scanning at the library
- www.faxzero.com fax 3 pages for free online
- Free classes at local hospitals
- Free printing at local unemployment agencies

Entertainment

I grew up with no TV and no home phone. Looking back I now know it was because we couldn't afford it. I read books, and listened to the radio. 98.1 FM Galax VA. NASCAR on Saturdays, Blue grass gospel on Sundays, and Adventures in Odyssey and Unshackled on Saturdays. Occasionally we'd make it to the City Park or library. If we didn't have that, there was always church & homework. I want to believe that the lack of outside entertainment made us kids more focused. Coming from single unemployed moms

& poverty we all graduated with 4 year degrees.

Colossians 3:17 - And whatsoever ye do in word or deed, [do] all in the name of the Lord Jesus, giving thanks to God and the Father by him.

- Library events
- YMCA scholarships based on income for the pool, sports ECT...
- Local Parks & Recreation calendar
- Local chamber of Commerce events & Visitors bureau events
- Local radio station events calendar
- Call all local attractions zoos, museums, galleries, theaters, etc... Ask if they have any FREE or discount days or if they offer EBT Food stamp or AAA discounts.
- Meetups.com
- Buy new movies at the flea market or rent them at the library
- Visit local pet stores, the beach or local parks
- Hospital event colanders and hospital classes
- Mega Church event calendars
- Tickets to local sporting events from scalpers
- Hulu.com, netflix.com, hbonow.com, dovechannel.com
- Megabus.com
- Timeshare vacations to Florida (Various locations) for $99 if you take their 3-4 hour tour

Christmas/ Thanksgiving

One of the best Thanksgiving holidays I remember was at my Aunt Lisa's house just before she passed away. Her broccoli casserole dish was the best. I'm grateful she shared the recipe with me. May she always be remembered.

Hebrews 13:8 Jesus Christ the same yesterday, and today, and forever.

- Marine Toys for Tots
- Salvation Army Christmas Angel tree

- Angel tree sign ups start as early as August and September
- Call Publix and get the date they will have free Thanksgiving & Christmas dinner in store
- Check the newspaper the week before thanksgiving and call local radio stations for a listing of free thanksgiving meals
- Call local food banks on November 1st and find out the sign up process for Thanksgiving food boxes
- Volunteer at a soup kitchen or non-profit and not only assist but eat for free
- Look for Christmas trees on craigslist during the Summer & Fall
- Attend free church Christmas concerts and plays fun for the whole family
- Shop for toys on clearance or high end thrift stores during the Spring and Summer and save it for Christmas
- Call thrift stores and ask what day they get donated items from stores like Target and JC Penny.
- Shop clearance at Hobby Lobby, Michaels, Target etc.... for holiday gifts

Credit/ Banking

Credit is my second love next to frugal living! Credit is your credibility and your key. What I learned as a "credit repair" specialist is that while tactics and loopholes exist to change a score or how something is reported, true transformation only occurs with a disciplined behavior change.

Luke 19:23 Whereforethen gavest not thou my money into the bank, that at my coming I might have required mine own with usury?

- www.creditkarma.com
- www.annualcreditreport.com
- Check your report for any negative items over 7 years old- request a deletion based on the 7 year time limit rule
- For any other credit corrections: Purchase my book "

Deleted"
- Order your chexsystems report at www.chexsystems.com
- For any corrections instructions order my book " Deleted"
- There are now several banks that will do business with individuals listed in chexsystems: Wood Forest, BOA second chance checking and many others offer second chance checking call and ask first
- If you have a problem with overdraft fees please consider declining overdraft protection. Its better something be declined than you have a $35 plus fee for something that put you $2 over

Miscellaneous: Things you can buy with EBT for multiple uses

When cash is short and you need to be wise.

Genesis 6:21 And take thou unto thee of all food that is eaten, and thou shalt gather it to thee; and it shall be for food for thee, and for them.

- Baking Soda- multiple uses
- Coconut oil, olive oil- hair grease, skin moisturizer, tooth ache remedy
- Food coloring- crafts
- Salt & Baking soda & water – insect bites
- Orange peel and Cinnamon sticks- boil for natural air fresheners
- Vinegar- gets rid of gnats
- Lemon juice- hair highlighter
- Vinegar, Baking Soda, Lemon juice- Cleaning agents
- Honey- Face wash mask
- Kerry Gold Butter- Ghee for hair moisturizer
- Flour, Salt, Food color- Play dough
- Goats Milk & Honey- Bath Soak
- Cornstarch- foot powder, baby powder

- Mayonnaise – dry hair
- Honey – for burns, zits
- Olive oil- polish shoes
- Lemon- removes fish smell from hands and arms
- Cinnamon- keeps slugs and snails away from seedlings
- Oatmeal- on dog or cat feces to make it dry and easier to clean
- Cold cabbage leaves- Lactation relieves blocked milk and soreness
- Cola- removes rust from pans
- Vinegar- cleans coffee machines if ran through the cycle
- Baking soda and coarse salt – cleans cast iron skillets
- Milk- cleans chocolate stains
- Salt with vinegar- weed killer
- Garlic cloves- earache
- Pasta shapes and colors- kids crafts
- Sticky rice- glue for kids crafts
- Peanut butter- gets rid of water rings on wood furniture

Miscellaneous

You live and you learn.

Ephesians 5: 15-16 See then that ye walk circumspectly, not as fools, but as wise, Redeeming the time, because the days are evil.

- UPS use AAA discount for printing
- Purchase high school booster discount cards for local merchant discounts
- When you need cash/credit fast go through your house and see if you have any new unused items you can return to a department store in exchange for a store gift card
- Retailmenot.com for online coupons
- Best discount cards to invest in: AAA, Student Advantage
- AMF gives free bowling on your birthday (call for details)
- Old Navy gives 10% off on your birthday
- AAA gives % off at New York & Company & Payless Shoes
- YMCA offers individual & family scholarships
- Invest in a pre-paid a debit card to use for on line purchases and rentals
- For extra cash you may be eligible for class action settlements www.topclassactions.com
- If you have a problem with late fee's DO NOT rent from libraries, redbox, or any other place that you can lose money to unnecessary late fees. Instead BUY books and movies at department stores, the flea market, the library, and yard sales. Also use Netflix and free books online.

Local City, State Notes Section, Local Contact Numbers

Local City, State Notes Section, Local Contact Numbers

Local City, State Notes Section, Local Contact Numbers

Local City, State Notes Section, Local Contact Numbers

Local City, State Notes Section, Local Contact Numbers

Local City, State Notes Section, Local Contact Numbers

Local City, State Notes Section, Local Contact Numbers

Local City, State Notes Section, Local Contact Numbers

Local City, State Notes Section, Local Contact Numbers

Local City, State Notes Section, Local Contact Numbers

Local City, State Notes Section, Local Contact Numbers

www.ingramcontent.com/pod-product-compliance
Lightning Source LLC
Chambersburg PA
CBHW070428190526
45169CB00003B/1456